REAL Conversations

The Operations Leader's Quick and Dirty Guide to Effective Employee Engagement

PHIL LOWER

DEDICATION

I've had the honor of leading front-line operations teams in two of my own businesses and several other organizations. An operations manager understands at a different, visceral level what corporate leaders, investors, and financial analysts sometimes struggle to understand – the real life impact of the business decisions made and how they affect the customer and their team.

Coincidentally, this is also the difference between most small and medium-sized business owners and their corporate counterparts. The budget is immediately affected by a corporate decision but families are affected by downturns in a small business.

This is not to minimize the emotional toll a leader in a Fortune, Inc., or a Business Insider company experiences when decisions about head count have to be made. I know for a fact that they struggle with hard decisions and the weight they carry on their shoulders and hearts. I know the pain of not making your sales numbers and how you ruminate about having to document your teammate's performance.

It is a very different feeling when you are eyeball to eyeball and you have to take the ass chewing from a customer you worked 5 years to get to know, someone dropped the ball, and now they are storming out of your office, or kicking you out of theirs, and you have to make payroll next week.

You small business owners,

You operations managers,

You front-line fighters,

YOU are my heroes.

You bring it to the fight every day and you take the good with the bad. Generals aren't awarded Medals of Honor.

You are.

This book is dedicated to every single one of you, to help you succeed in a faster, more challenging world.

All my best,

Phil Lower

CONTENTS

Dedication i

Acknowlegements v

Introduction 1

Start With Better Questions 3

The Two Paradoxes of Employee Engagement 7

The Essence of Leadership 13

The Rule of 15 15

Conclusion 21

Notes 24

About the Author 27

ACKNOWLEDGMENTS

To Lei, Dani, and Gabi for encouraging me
to step up and into who I could become.

Sandy Chernoff, Eddie Velez, and Brian Kennedy,
I cherish your years of support and friendship.

Thank you Chris Cayer for editing my work and for
repeatedly being a great sounding board for my creativity
and ideas. You have one of the most brilliant minds.

INTRODUCTION

"In the end, it's about the teaching, and what I always loved about coaching was the practice. Not the games, not the tournaments, not the alumni stuff. But teaching the players during practice was what coaching was all about to me."

- John Wooden

REAL Conversations is based on real-world, practical execution, coaching techniques, and experiences managing operational teams that needed to succeed in order to eat.

There are many coaching schools of thought and industry "best practices" that are useful for different types of coaching situations. But, as a leader at any level of an organization, where do you learn them?

There is an overabundance of Executive and Leadership coaches, that have in fact, never lead an organization or team of any significant size. In other words, they can ask great questions, but they can't relate to the gravity of the decisions that result from those answers. And, there are very few Operations-level coaches because many companies don't value or can't afford the expense of 1-on-1 coaching to develop their bench strength.

Therefore, the Operations Leader, in order to grow and be promoted, either has to earn their degree through the School of Hard Knocks, has to personally pay for that growth and development, has to somehow miraculously figure it out, or they need a senior leader that is willing to invest part of their precious time as a mentor and coach.

Fortunately, more and more Regional and District-level managers are spending their weekly meetings in group coaching with their teams while they pour through their metrics, goals, and challenges. But how does an Operational Manager implement techniques, policies and procedures, and achieve their goals day to day? How do you energize already >65% of passively engaged and actively disengaged employees? How do you win when generations are changing and so are their expectations and values?

REAL Conversations helps fill in that gap. So, let's get to the Bottom Line. You've got enough to do today.

START WITH BETTER QUESTIONS

"Management teams aren't good at asking questions. In business
school, we train them to be good at giving answers."

– Clayton M. Christensen

One of the dynamics of leadership is that focused leaders rise
to the top. The question must then be asked, "What are they
focused on?" Tricky question. Based on an individual's
personality style and natural biases, they answer the
question and act according to their archetype.

Psychology 101.

When you attend a meeting, what do they tend to be about?
Metrics, Money and Numbers. Why? You can't target a goal
that you can't see and you only measure things that are
important to you. Numbers facilitate that in every way.

The average meeting goes like this:

> We are spending $350,000 annually on training.

> Your technician turnover rate is 78%.

> Your average employee tenure is 9 months, but we
> break even at 18.

> What are YOU doing wrong?

Few proceed in the following way:

> We are spending $350,000 annually on training.

> Our technician turnover rate is 78%.

> Our average employee tenure is 9 months, but we break even at 18.

> What are WE doing wrong?

> Are employee productivity and performance metrics improving, stagnant, or declining?

> Are these trends cyclical or seasonal? Or, could they be an indicator of something we need to address?

> What causes employees to leave our company?

> Do employees feel connected to our company in other aspects of their lives?

> Do employees see how their role within our company furthers their own career goals?

> How do employees feel about our company leadership?

> How do employees feel about their direct managers?

> What are our Glassdoor or Yelp reviews saying about our company?

> Out of our identified high potential employees, how many have expressed an interest in additional training, whether inside or outside the company?

> When was the last time that training request was approved and how much did it cost? How do we track the ROI on that training cost?

> How frequently are we updating our company metrics?

> Can we pull up Daily, Weekly, Monthly, Quarterly metrics whenever we want?

> How many different ways do we recognize our team

members?

Are there any other costs we are not capturing that help us see the real value of investing more in our team?

There are so many more great quality questions that need to be asked. The better the quality of the questions asked, the better the results you'll achieve.

THE TWO PARADOXES OF EMPLOYEE ENGAGEMENT

"Today, no leader can afford to be indifferent to the challenge of engaging employees in the work of creating the future. Engagement may have been optional in the past, but it's pretty much the whole game today."

– Gary Hamel

Paradox #1 – "Show me the money" or Show me results and I'll spend more money to get you better results.

Typically, the lie is: If we had more money, we'd spend it on these "pet" projects. The reality is that the money would be spent elsewhere based on the organizational power struggles, dynamics, and priorities.

Now, in light of Paradox #1, how do you kill the engagement dragon? Answer: Have genuine empathy for your team. In other words, actually care about them outside of work. I'm not saying spend time with them at a bar because that can cross an ethical boundary.

Employees leave bad managers faster than bad companies. Why? Often because they will tolerate a rarely used policy and procedure out of ignorance but a bad manager is in their space daily.

Therefore, make sure your open door is actually open and so is your heart. Great leaders are in touch with their humanity. They also facilitate their teammates' success. If they don't, they're setting them up for empty promises and emotional abuse based on the repeated rollercoaster ride of unfulfilled expectations, hopes, and dreams.

Paradox #2 – The Cream Rises to the Top. The reality of this is that those managers that focus on money, numbers, and metrics (more than people), traditionally, have been more frequently promoted because they achieve results according to the most commonly used metrics. Yet, this still leaves the other viable questions and metrics on the table.

Furthermore, it reinforces the Peter Principle since technically competent managers rise to a certain level. But, in order to grow further, you must become a leader of teams.

Addressing the Pair of Doxes

The answer to both paradoxes is EQ. Empathy towards customer difficulties, teammate struggles, your own internal voice and limiting beliefs, as the Ops Leader in the fight, your emotional intelligence resolves both problems because it bridges the gap between productivity/goal attainment and employee/team engagement.

One of the tools I developed to help Operations Leaders (especially those that are more interpersonally reserved) build more engaged teams is a conversational coaching and development methodology called REAL Conversations.

    R = Reality
    E = Expectation
    A = Adversity
    L = Looking Forward

What Do REAL Conversations Achieve?

When a manager needs to have a discussion about performance issues, frequently business needs and time constraints necessitate a quick and dirty conversation. The poorest quality ones are frequently one-sided. The highest quality often start with the accomplishments and then progress to obstacles. But, from my experience, coaching and training business owners and managers, these higher quality conversations are few and far between.

REAL offers a simple, replicable methodology that anyone can follow because it progresses naturally, grows leader EQ, and improves team cohesion.

"Employee Engagement = ROI" – Phil Lower

Reality

What do you know about your teammate's market, job requirements, life outside of work? What is their competition doing to take their accounts? What regulatory or company policy changes might they be facing?

Ask yourself, "How would I change my conversation style if my friend just lost his dog?" Why wouldn't I treat my colleague or direct report with the same sympathy?

Checking into someone else's reality requires the Operations Leader to express sincere interest in their direct reports. For some personality styles (the more task oriented and metrics driven) this is where they will stumble.

Walking a mile in someone else's shoes is precisely why Reality is the first thing to developing EQ and employee engagement. People are always thinking about themselves and WIIFM (What's in it for me?). Showing sincere appreciation for another person's life builds rapport and relationship.

When you begin your meeting, pull the reigns back before

diving into your spreadsheet. Simply ask, "How's everything going?", and then remain silent. Let the answer guide the conversation. The team mate that is also money, numbers, and metrics oriented will drive the conversation towards the meeting goal. The others can be brought around in the next step.

Expectation

We all have goals to achieve, WIIFM to pursue, bills to pay, and vacations we want to take. Life is full of give and take, sowing and reaping, and income from your customers or employer help facilitate this.

What people holding the purse strings expect you to accomplish for them determines whether or not you get paid.

After you begin your REAL Conversation with discovering your team member's Reality, ask them for the Expectation they needed to achieve. Provided they know, or can reference it, take the next step of discussing their achievement or lack thereof.

- What are their immediate money, number, metrics goals vs achievements?
- What progress have they made towards a larger goal?
- Is the larger goal sufficiently broken down into smaller goals and performance-based tasks, to be measured in the current time frame?
- How are you measuring their progress towards program or project completion?
- What unforeseen obstacles slowed them down, and what expected obstacles were bigger in real life than they appeared in earlier stages?

Once you've uncovered their present state vs expected state, you can problem solve expected and potential adversities they will encounter.

Adversity

Two of the essential functions of a leader are to supply the needs of their team and to remove obstacles from their path.

Once you've reviewed present state against Expectation, open the door to discussing:

- The different challenges they have already overcome,
- Those that are immediately visible, and
- The potential pitfalls before them.

Take notes. From my experience, this is the moment when you will begin seeing which teammates are actively engaged, passively engaged, and actively disengaged.

How do they reveal themselves? Very easily, actually.

Engaged, growth-minded people answer with explanations, solutions, problems they confronted and defeated, positive achievements, and other, results-oriented answers.

Passive and disengaged individuals focus almost solely on the problems or don't have solution-oriented action steps to work on. They're not actively looking for things to improve, that could pose risks going forward, let alone the current risks staring at them in their present role.

They're not growth minded.

As an Operational Leader, the biggest hurdle you may have here is your own bias. This is why it is vitally important for you to start with Reality. Start anywhere else and you lose the humanity and relational understanding you gain that will help you drive productivity.

The incremental gain found in improving an actively engaged employee's performance can't be undervalued. However, turning a single passively engaged team member into an actively engaged participant can dramatically shift your numbers in a very short time.

Looking Forward

We all want recognition for a job well done. We want to know that what we did made a difference and that what we are working towards will have a lasting impact. Here's where it happens and/or is projected to happen.

- If a person is misaligned in their role, alignment happens here.
- If a person is working towards a career goal, alignment happens here.
- If a person is wondering how what they are doing fits into the bigger scheme of things, alignment happens here.

Looking Forward is about seeing into the horizon and steering the ship in that direction.

As an Ops Leader that knows their team, this is where you help them see what they are doing is aligning with the organizational Mission, Vision, Values, and Strategic Goals. This is where they can see Divisional, Regional, and District alignment. But, this is where your familiarity with their personal aspirations (WIIFM) is aligned to the organization and their paycheck.

Here is the opportunity to reinforce positive, productive behavior and recognize achievement with their WIIFM. Here is where you water and fertilize their positive psychology and ask for commitment on just one or two additional steps they can improve over the next relevant time frame.

Commitment is King. People don't like to back out on promises they make unless they are lying to you.

And, just like that, you've now brought them full circle from their Reality and into alignment with the larger goals, or the exit door. Either way, you get to make your team into the group of high achievers you want to work with.

THE ESSENCE OF LEADERSHIP

"You can identify them by their fruit, that is, by the way they act. Can you pick grapes from thorn bushes, or figs from thistles?" – St Matthew 7:16, NLT

"Belief that influences behavior influences results."

– Tom Herman

Our beliefs govern our behavior. What you believe about a person, place or thing, influences how you treat them or it.

The Essence of Leadership is conveying our beliefs, by demonstrating our behaviors, and reinforcing those beliefs and expected behaviors for those we lead.

We measure manager performance because study after study shows that poor management causes poor team performance. Moreover, both executives and employees surveyed rank managers as increasingly incompetent over the last 30 years. One of the critical reasons why is that most leaders don't have a roadmap they can share with managers of what behaviors produce positive results and ultimately positive and productive employee engagement.

"The floggings will continue until morale improves."

– Anonymous

Allow me to clarify this point.

If the leadership in an organization behaves in such a way that is incongruent with their stated beliefs and values, then everyone in that organization will eventually recognize the hypocrisy. Turnover will be high, Glassdoor and Yelp reviews will stink, profits will eventually be lower than necessary, and secondary costs related to stress and team disengagement will increase.

On the other hand, if leadership believes in certain principles, and reflects those beliefs in their behaviors, they will also be aligned in their values, able to express them confidently, and achieve results accordingly.

Why is a company like EvolveIP able to retain an astounding 90% of their IT team? Their Founders and leaders live and reinforce their core beliefs and behaviors daily.

EvolveIP's Company Values very closely resemble the research I've done.

I call it The Rule of 15.

THE RULE OF 15

"Back in the day, what motivated me was overcoming myself. Now I believe in being a leader. I've done it all – I'm good. Now, it's about setting an example for others to follow. I can't just talk it – I have to live it." – David Goggins

"Let the elders who rule well be counted worthy of double honor."

– 1 Timothy 5:17, NKJV

There are 15 universal Rules, that when they are demonstrated, result in higher productivity, stronger employee engagement, and a richer life experience at and away from work. They are:

Rule	Behavior
1. Listen First, Speak Last	Give people the opportunity to render their opinion, or share their concern, before you speak. Listen and seek to understand their position, opinion, or motivation before sharing your opinion. Only ask questions to clarify your understanding before sharing your opinion. Do not ask questions to manipulate their position or change their opinion.

2. Speak Clearly	Use simple language that anyone can understand. Whenever possible, don't hide behind industry or corporate jargon. Also, be honest and tell the truth instead of sugar coating something. That doesn't excuse you from being tactful or diplomatic. But, don't run from calling things as you see them without using manipulation and influencing others in an inappropriate manner.
3. Model Respect	People won't care until they know you care about them. Be genuine and care about their dignity and their person. Treat everyone with respect. If integrity is doing the right thing even when no one is looking, then giving respect is important even when someone can't do anything for you. Show kindness and practice doing the little things that build people up.
4. Be Transparent	Can you be fact checked? Have you provided the means for people to confirm what you're saying independently? Can you be reviewed by peers and do you review them? Do you set the bar for clarity and openness? Is your input sincere and genuine? Or, are you trying to manipulate the situation or people to your advantage?
5. Engage Reality	Team members and customers have their own perception of reality. Engage with them and offer technical or emotional support whenever possible. Give compassion and empathy equal space to money and numbers goals.

5 (continued)	Diffuse conflict with empathy and appropriate use of company policies. Be willing to have tough conversations when necessary.
6. Set Clear Expectations	Understand and communicate needs and expectations as clearly as possible. Ask check questions to confirm understanding. As it arises, clear out as much vagueness and confusion as possible. Be available to offer help and ask if there are any questions, or points of confusion, frequently, without micromanaging. The 17" across baseball Home Plate has never changed at any level of play, for any player's level of performance. Everybody knows where they stand. It's universal.
7. Model Smart Trust	Learn the skills and talents of your team. Extend trust intelligently based on those skills and talents. Grow your trust by testing it with new projects that you support but don't micromanage. Add other experienced team members to a working group that can support the leader without taking it over. Ask them to mentor the team leader when necessary. Focus on the reward of success without overemphasizing the risk of failure. Celebrate lessons learned from wins and losses.

8. Model Loyalty	Your team is most important. Give them the credit for your successes liberally and generously. Own the failures and protect them at all cost. Limit favoritism. Make sure they share the glory with others. Defend against bullies, no matter how high their position. Do not tolerate gossip and backbiting. Have a clearly defined Code of Conduct and/or Code of Ethics, both in written documents, which each and every team member must sign on to, and issue them, updated as needed, on a regular basis.
9. Follow Through on Commitments	Appraise the need, situation, or project and state your requirements for handling it clearly. Then, do what you commit to. If something changes, communicate it immediately, especially if the change will affect your commitment. Don't be afraid to ask for more resources when they would help you keep the commitment.
10. Model Accountability	Be accountable for your results and help others be accountable for theirs. Take personal responsibility and instill personal responsibility in others. Celebrate their good behavior and results publicly and have private conversations about deficits. When others point out your failures, don't run from them.
11. Do the Right Thing	When you make a mistake, own it and learn the lesson well. When someone else is weak in an area, cause as little pain as possible. Humility is a sign of personal strength. If you offend someone, apologize

11 (continued)	quickly. The customer is not always right. But, they pay the bills. So, take care of them as best you can and go the extra mile whenever possible.
12. Continuously Improve	Be a lifelong learner and support others growth personally and professionally. Seek ways to provide them with the resources and opportunities to grow. Look for multiple mentors, or a mastermind group, to help you improve different aspects of your own development. Create a positive, constructive feedback loop and act upon what you receive. And, make sure that you instill, nurture, and develop these values in each and every one of your teammates.
13. Produce Results	Break long-term goals and initiatives into the smallest tasks and goals possible. Tackle them as quickly as possible and track your progress. Hit the hardest tasks first. Note milestones and adjust your Critical Path as necessary. Only promise what you can deliver and follow-through on. When you face a roadblock, seek help to overcome it. Delegate where possible.
14. Foster Diversity	Proactively seek out information and opinions from people of different cultural, demographic backgrounds, and personality styles. Express others' value in conversation with sincere examples whenever appropriate. Consider what it takes to have the best team rather than personal comfort or familiarity.

15. Be Adaptable	Be willing to try new things (and even old things that failed) when new technology or circumstances might change the outcome. Roll with the punches and reduce your frustration at people, places, processes, and policies by communicating the "Why" so people don't add to your stress and adapt with you.

CONCLUSION

"I had no idea that being your authentic self could make me as rich as I've become. If I had, I'd have done it a lot earlier."

- Oprah Winfrey

The magic word is Authenticity.

Teams that spend 40-50 hours per week together are often more like a family than you are with your extended family and siblings.

Employees want leaders that lead them, support them, and take the fire with them.

Show genuine appreciation and interest, and your team will follow you into the Valley of the Shadow of Death because they know you will lead them through to the other side.

Your interest is reflected in your manner and content of conversation with your team. They will smell a phony coming a mile away.

Ultimately, it seems pretty straightforward. You have three options.

1. Demonstrate these behaviors because you believe in their worth, will live towards these values, and will hold others accountable for them, as well.

2. Don't behave according to the Rules, and don't hold people accountable for productive behaviors, and not be as

successful as those who do.

3. Don't behave according to the Rules, yet hold other people accountable when they don't either, and let your hypocrisy be revealed.

Since you reap what you sow, follow this 7 Step Process:

1. Start by asking better questions that will move your team forward.

2. Assess your actual leaderships' behaviors, not just touchy feely pulse surveys that your managers coach their teams to answer.

3. Create a bi-weekly or monthly coachable format and narrative that everyone adheres to, including at minimum, a Code of Conduct. Review raw metrics, present challenges, opportunities, and future risks.

4. Develop systems that can produce daily metrics, accessible at a moment's notice.

5. Reassess your leaders' behaviors every quarter moving forward. Watch for trends.

6. Compare your performance metrics and leaders' behaviors against history and adjust coaching and training as needed.

7. Find better questions to ask.

By following these steps, you're going to have so many great opportunities to drive engagement and increase productivity.

I created REAL Conversations to give Operations leaders a simple tool they could easily adopt, adapt to their specific team needs, and achieve better results faster.

No matter what industry you're in, and even if you're not an operational level leader, if you've read this far, bet on yourself and your team, because I am. I'm looking forward to seeing you and your team in the winner's circle.

Feel free to connect with my team or myself if you ever have any questions about how to implement these ideas, assessments, or methodologies, in a practical manner, for your unique situation.

Email: **info@paladincoaching.com** or connect with me on LinkedIn.

NOTES

ABOUT THE AUTHOR

Phil Lower founded Paladin Coaching and specializes in Leadership Development and Employee Engagement, by building impactful training programs that drive ROI. He speaks about personal responsibility, emotional resilience, and a leader's spirit.

He is a Certified Professional Coach having coached, mentored, and trained professionals from 30 different countries. He has trained leaders in Fortune 500 companies, small business owners, and independent professionals.

Phil's background includes serving as a Director on the Board of a human services company, being the college Chair of a Liberal Arts Department, as well as leadership, consulting, and operations roles with Fortune 1000 Firms.

Phil authored Dad Quote of the Day: Wit and Wisdom of a Strong Coffee Drinking Dad and also founded Dad Quote of the Day (#DQOTD) to create an ecosystem of products and services where profits go to help families that are confronting homelessness.